YouTube Planning Book for Kids

This Planner Belongs to

. . . .

FROM THIS BOOK YOU WILL LEARN

- HOW TO START A YOUTUBE CHANNEL
- HOW TO PLAN EACH VIDEO SET GOALS FOR YOURSELF
- HAVE · FUN WHILE CREATING CONTENT

- THIS BOOK WILL

- MOTIVATE YOU TO GROW YOUR CHANNEL
- GUIDE YOU TO EACH STEP OF THE PROCESS
- ORGANIZE IDEAS
- MUCH MORE...

CONTENT BRAINSTORMING

Before you start your channel make sure you have a clear idea...start by asking yourself a few questions:

- What is your channel going to be about?

- ....

- What topic do you know well?

- ....

- What type of content do I enjoy? (Vlogs, tutorials, reviews, entertainment.)

- ....

- How much time each week can I dedicate to video production?

- ....

- Who is going to be the target of my videos?

- ....

INSPIRATION AND IDEAS

<u>Write below</u> what inspires you, what other channels you enjoy watching, what are the most important things a channel should have?

What do you usually look for in a channel?

How to start a YouTube Channel

Create your account

- First, you need to create a Gmail email address
- Sign into YouTube and click on the user icon at the top right of the screen.
- Click on the gear icon to get to your account's Settings
- Click on Create a new channel
- Then choose "Use a business or other name"
- Add your Brand name and click create
- Fill out your profile and channel
- description Optimize your video for search (use relevant keywords that are already used by the viewers)
- Create a catchy title
- Upload your first video

TO DO LIST

DECIDE THE TOPIC OF THE CHANNEL

DECIDE THE STYLE OF THE CHANNEL

DECIDE THE NAME OF THE CHANNEL

TO DO LIST

HOW WILL YOU SHOT THE VIDEOS?
(VIDEO CAMERA, SCREENCAST.)

HOW WILL YOU EDIT THE VIDEOS
(WHAT SOFTWARE DO I NEED?)
(RECOMMENDED PROGRAM: WINDOWS MOVIE
MAKER)

THUMBNAILS CREATION
(RECOMMENDED PROGRAM: CANVA)

MY GOAL FOR THE FIRST MONTH

MY GOAL FOR THE SIX MONTHS

MY GOAL FOR THE FIRST YEAR

 # REMEMBER

DON'T FOCUS TOO MUCH ON THE VIDEO QUALITY AND EDITING, THINK MORE ABOUT THE CONTENT OF THE CHANNEL, AND THE WAY IT IS PRESENTED

DON'T GET FRUSTRATED IF YOUR VIDEOS HAVE ZERO VIEWS, IT TAKES TIME AND CONSISTENCY TO LET A CHANNEL GROW

PRODUCE MORE VIDEOS!
PRODUCE MORE VIDEOS!
PRODUCE MORE VIDEOS!

CREATE QUALITY CONTENT

INVITE TO SUBSCRIBE AND SHARE YOUR VIDEO!

ENGAGE WITH YOUR SUBSCRIBERS BY ASKING THEM QUESTIONS AND OPINIONS

DAY _____ VIDEO #N _____

VIDEO TITLE _____

What is the topic of this video?

_____

_____

_____

_____

What will happen in this video? (How should you start it? What will be in the middle? How will it end?)

_____

_____

_____

_____

_____

_____

_____

DAY _____ **VIDEO #N** _____

VIDEO TITLE _____

What is the topic of this video?

_____

_____

_____

_____

What will happen in this video? (How should you start it? What will be in the middle? How will it end?)

_____

_____

_____

_____

_____

_____

DAY _____ **VIDEO #N** _____

VIDEO TITLE _____

What is the topic of this video?

_____

_____

_____

_____

What will happen in this video? (How should you start it? What will be in the middle? How will it end?)

_____

_____

_____

_____

_____

_____

_____

DAY _____   VIDEO #N _____

VIDEO TITLE _____

What is the topic of this video?

_____

_____

_____

_____

What will happen in this video? (How should you start it? What will be in the middle? How will it end?)

_____

_____

_____

_____

_____

_____

_____

_____

DAY _____   VIDEO #N _____

VIDEO TITLE _____

What is the topic of this video?

_____

_____

_____

_____

What will happen in this video? (How should you start it? What will be in the middle? How will it end?)

_____

_____

_____

_____

_____

_____

_____

DAY _____ **VIDEO #N** _____

VIDEO TITLE _____

What is the topic of this video?

_____

_____

_____

_____

What will happen in this video? (How should you start it? What will be in the middle? How will it end?)

_____

_____

_____

_____

_____

_____

_____

DAY _____ VIDEO #N _____

VIDEO TITLE _____

What is the topic of this video?

_____

_____

_____

_____

What will happen in this video? (How should you start it? What will be in the middle? How will it end?)

_____

_____

_____

_____

_____

_____

_____

DAY _____ VIDEO #N

VIDEO TITLE

What is the topic of this video?

What will happen in this video? (How should you start it? What will be in the middle? How will it end?)

DAY _____ **VIDEO #N** _____

VIDEO TITLE _____

What is the topic of this video?

_____

_____

_____

What will happen in this video? (How should you start it? What will be in the middle? How will it end?)

_____

_____

_____

_____

_____

_____

_____

DAY   **VIDEO #N**

VIDEO TITLE

What is the topic of this video?

What will happen in this video? (How should you start it? What will be in the middle? How will it end?)

DAY _____ VIDEO #N _____

VIDEO TITLE _____

What is the topic of this video?

_____

_____

_____

_____

What will happen in this video? (How should you start it? What will be in the middle? How will it end?)

_____

_____

_____

_____

_____

_____

_____

DAY _____ **VIDEO #N** _____

VIDEO TITLE _____

What is the topic of this video?

_____

_____

_____

_____

What will happen in this video? (How should you start it? What will be in the middle? How will it end?)

_____

_____

_____

_____

_____

_____

DAY _____ **VIDEO #N** _____

VIDEO TITLE _____

What is the topic of this video?

_____

_____

_____

_____

What will happen in this video? (How should you start it? What will be in the middle? How will it end?)

_____

_____

_____

_____

_____

_____

_____

DAY   **VIDEO #N**

VIDEO TITLE

What is the topic of this video?

What will happen in this video? (How should you start it? What will be in the middle? How will it end?)

DAY _____ VIDEO #N _____

VIDEO TITLE _____

What is the topic of this video?

_____

_____

_____

_____

What will happen in this video? (How should you start it? What will be in the middle? How will it end?)

_____

_____

_____

_____

_____

_____

_____

DAY _____ **VIDEO #N** _____

VIDEO TITLE _____

What is the topic of this video?

_____

_____

_____

_____

What will happen in this video? (How should you start it? What will be in the middle? How will it end?)

_____

_____

_____

_____

_____

_____

_____

DAY _____   VIDEO #N _____

VIDEO TITLE _____

What is the topic of this video?

What will happen in this video? (How should you start it? What will be in the middle? How will it end?)

DAY _____ VIDEO #N _____

VIDEO TITLE _____

What is the topic of this video?

_____

_____

_____

_____

What will happen in this video? (How should you start it? What will be in the middle? How will it end?)

_____

_____

_____

_____

_____

_____

_____

DAY _____ VIDEO #N _____

VIDEO TITLE

What is the topic of this video?

_____

_____

_____

_____

What will happen in this video? (How should you start it? What will be in the middle? How will it end?)

_____

_____

_____

_____

_____

_____

_____

DAY _____ **VIDEO #N** _____

VIDEO TITLE _____

What is the topic of this video?

_____

_____

_____

_____

What will happen in this video? (How should you start it? What will be in the middle? How will it end?)

_____

_____

_____

_____

_____

_____

_____

DAY _____ **VIDEO #N** _____

VIDEO TITLE _____

What is the topic of this video?

_____

_____

_____

_____

What will happen in this video? (How should
you start it? What will be in the middle? How
will it end?)

_____

_____

_____

_____

_____

_____

_____

DAY _____ **VIDEO #N** _____

VIDEO TITLE _____

What is the topic of this video?

_____

_____

_____

_____

What will happen in this video? (How should you start it? What will be in the middle? How will it end?)

_____

_____

_____

_____

_____

_____

DAY _____ **VIDEO #N** _____

VIDEO TITLE _____

What is the topic of this video?

What will happen in this video? (How should you start it? What will be in the middle? How will it end?)

DAY _____ VIDEO #N _____

VIDEO TITLE _____

What is the topic of this video?

_____

_____

_____

_____

What will happen in this video? (How should
you start it? What will be in the middle? How
will it end?)

_____

_____

_____

_____

_____

_____

DAY ＿＿＿＿＿ VIDEO #N ＿＿＿＿＿

VIDEO TITLE ＿＿＿＿＿

What is the topic of this video?

＿＿＿＿＿＿＿＿＿＿＿＿＿＿＿＿＿＿

＿＿＿＿＿＿＿＿＿＿＿＿＿＿＿＿＿＿

＿＿＿＿＿＿＿＿＿＿＿＿＿＿＿＿＿＿

＿＿＿＿＿＿＿＿＿＿＿＿＿＿＿＿＿＿

What will happen in this video? (How should you start it? What will be in the middle? How will it end?)

＿＿＿＿＿＿＿＿＿＿＿＿＿＿＿＿＿＿

＿＿＿＿＿＿＿＿＿＿＿＿＿＿＿＿＿＿

＿＿＿＿＿＿＿＿＿＿＿＿＿＿＿＿＿＿

＿＿＿＿＿＿＿＿＿＿＿＿＿＿＿＿＿＿

＿＿＿＿＿＿＿＿＿＿＿＿＿＿＿＿＿＿

＿＿＿＿＿＿＿＿＿＿＿＿＿＿＿＿＿＿

DAY _____ VIDEO #N _____

VIDEO TITLE _____

What is the topic of this video?

_____

_____

_____

_____

What will happen in this video? (How should you start it? What will be in the middle? How will it end?)

_____

_____

_____

_____

_____

_____

_____

DAY _____ VIDEO #N _____

VIDEO TITLE _____

What is the topic of this video?

_____

_____

_____

_____

What will happen in this video? (How should
you start it? What will be in the middle? How
will it end?)

_____

_____

_____

_____

_____

_____

_____

DAY _____ VIDEO #N _____

VIDEO TITLE _____

What is the topic of this video?

_____

_____

_____

_____

What will happen in this video? (How should you start it? What will be in the middle? How will it end?)

_____

_____

_____

_____

_____

_____

_____

DAY _____ **VIDEO #N** _____

VIDEO TITLE _____

What is the topic of this video?

_____

_____

_____

_____

What will happen in this video? (How should you start it? What will be in the middle? How will it end?)

_____

_____

_____

_____

_____

_____

_____

DAY _____ VIDEO #N _____

VIDEO TITLE _____

What is the topic of this video?

_____

_____

_____

What will happen in this video? (How should
you start it? What will be in the middle? How
will it end?)

_____

_____

_____

_____

_____

_____

_____

_____

DAY _____ VIDEO #N _____

VIDEO TITLE

What is the topic of this video?

_____

_____

_____

_____

What will happen in this video? (How should you start it? What will be in the middle? How will it end?)

_____

_____

_____

_____

_____

_____

_____

DAY _____ **VIDEO #N** _____

VIDEO TITLE _____

What is the topic of this video?

_____

_____

_____

_____

What will happen in this video? (How should
you start it? What will be in the middle? How
will it end?)

_____

_____

_____

_____

_____

_____

_____

DAY _____ **VIDEO #N** _____

VIDEO TITLE _____

What is the topic of this video?

_____

_____

_____

_____

What will happen in this video? (How should
you start it? What will be in the middle? How
will it end?)

_____

_____

_____

_____

_____

_____

10 AMAZING FACTS
ABOUT
YOUTUBE

1. YouTube was founded on February 14th, 2005 by three ex-PayPal employees.

2. The first ever YouTube video was uploaded on April 23, 2005. By the co-founder at the San Diego Zoo.

3. Initially, YouTube was created to be a video dating site called "Tune In Hook Up."

4. Only 18 months after YouTube was founded, Google bought it for $1.65 billion in stocks.

5. There are over one billion users on YouTube, which is nearly one-third of everyone on the Internet.

6. Every minute, over 100 hours of video is uploaded to YouTube.

7. Every month, YouTubers watch 6 billion hours of v i d e o s per month, and 4 billion videos every day.

8. The first world leader to create a YouTube channel was the British Prime Minister, Tony Blair who made his account in 2007.

9. The longest video on YouTube is 571 hours, 1 minute, and 41 seconds long. That's the same as 23 days and 19 hours!

10. The first video that reached 1 billion views the fastest was Hello by Adele. It reached 1 billion views in 88 days.

 # REMEMBER

YOU DON'T HAVE TO BE PERFECT!!!

JUST CREATE CONTENT YOU WILL IMPROVE WITH EXPERIENCE AND BY MAKING MISTAKES

CREATING VIDEO MUST BE FUN, IF YOU ARE GETTING  STRESSED OUT, TAKE YOUR TIME!

BE CONSISTENT WITH YOUR CONTENTS START BY UPLOADING A VIDEO ONCE A WEEK

INVOLVE YOUR FRIENDS AND FAMILY!

GET CREATIVE!

IMPORTANT NOTES

WHAT I HAVE LEARNED

IMPORTANT NOTES

WHAT I HAVE LEARNED

Your channel is going strong!

Don't stop!

It will grow steadily and slowly!

Printed in Great Britain
by Amazon